Cathedral Forest by Charles Beck

Mortal Stakes | Faint Thunder

Mortal Stakes | Faint Thunder

new poems by

TIMOTHY MURPHY

2002 – 2009

Foreword by Clay S. Jenkinson

Preface by X. J. Kennedy

The Dakota Institute Press
of the Lewis & Clark Fort Mandan Foundation

Library of Congress Control Number 2011926189
ISBN-13 978-0-9825597-6-5 (Hardcover)
ISBN-13 978-0-9825597-7-2 (Paperback)

Distributed by The University of Oklahoma Press
Created, produced and designed in the United States of America
Printed in Canada

Book layout and design by:
Margaret McCullough corvusdesignstudio.com

The paper in this book meets the guidelines for permanence and durability of the Committee of Production Guidelines for Book Longevity of the Council on Library Resources.
10 9 8 7 6 5 4 3 2 1

Cover Image: Cathedral Forest *by Charles Beck*

The Dakota Institute Press
of the Lewis & Clark Fort Mandan Foundation
2576 8th Street South West . Post Office Box 607
Washburn, North Dakota 58577
www.fortmandan.com
1.877.462.8535

MIX
Paper from
responsible sources
FSC® C016245

FOREWORD

I have had the good fortune of going hunting with Tim Murphy. He's as passionate about killing birds as he is about writing poetry. More, perhaps. He's not like Massachusetts Senator John Kerry donning designer camouflage and a brand-spanking cap a few days before the 2004 presidential election to prove that he understood the soul of the American heartland. Murphy's gun is well worn, casually stowed in the red Ford Escape, a natural fit in his thin, strong arms. He rejected his brother's Subaru with hauteur as inadequate for this hunt. His hunting clothes are threadbare and patched, a huge tear in the right thigh—the fisher king's wound—hand-stitched back together on some endless winter night a few years ago. As we sat in a convenience store in Lisbon, North Dakota, gabbing and sipping after our fruitless hunt, he was indistinguishable, aside from his freckled face and rust-red hair, from other men who came in to pee or buy a soda. Except that as they blundered past us to get to the men's room or the window de-icer and Armor All, Murphy was cheerfully reciting his poems at a volume that must have startled anyone who had ears to listen. If they had paused to hear him out, for he writes mostly short and deceptively simple poems, they would have said, "Hey, this guy makes sense." Murphy doesn't go into some kind of ponderous vatic mode when he recites. He just recites, in the same tone he'd use if he were going through drive through.

Our hunt was organized as a video shoot for a short documentary film of the poet as Dakota pheasant hunter. It soon became clear to me, however, that our poet was far less interested in the video than in getting his share of North Dakota's pheasants. At one point, I asked him to turn and recite one of his poems for the camera. He half-turned, gave me a withering look, and said, "Later." I trudged behind him through 10 inches of snow for two or three miles while he worked his mayhem. When I fell through the ice of a slough and got my leg wet up to my pelvis, a dangerous accident on a seriously cold day in December on the treeless Great Plains, he made it clear that I could walk back to the car to get warm if I wished, but that I would be making that walk alone. I lurched after him with one pant leg frozen like the tin woodman. You get so few moments like this in a lifetime: nothing would have induced me to weasel back to the car.

Murphy is a curious mix of commoner and laureate. He will freely tell you that he is a serious poet whose work entitles him to occupy the same sentence with Robert Frost. Usually, a poet who will tell you that is insufferably insufferable. But when he says that wild thing it does not sound insane or merely pathetic, although it should be unbearable to hear any poet of the early twenty-first century invoke the word *Frost*. Murphy is completely humble about almost everything else in his life. His satisfaction with his poetic genius seems matter of fact rather than assertive or insecure. He tells you he talks a couple of times per week on the phone with Richard Wilbur, whom he regards as one of the greatest poets of the 20th century. Just tells you that while loading a shell into his shotgun, and as he speaks it is not name-dropping. He calls Wilbur his lodestar.

That's the curious thing about Tim Murphy. I've known a few serious poets in my time. They invariably behave as if Apollo made an early appearance at the foot of their bed, and they are surprised that we have not yet been made aware of that interesting fact. They wear the postmodern garb of the tribe. They have poets' severe tastes. They sport trophy dogs, who never worked a day in their life. Not Murphy. He's as likely as not talking about how America's love affair with ethanol drove the price of corn through the roof and bankrupted his hog operation. When an interviewer asks him about whether he suffers from the "anxiety of influence," he says, perhaps truthfully, *no*, and then he piles it on a little by saying that *anxiety of influence* "is a phrase whose provenance I don't even know." I was with him until *provenance*. And then, because he is feeling merely perverse, he adds, "I can hardly order dinner in French, and my favorite politician is Richard Cheney!"

It is not easy to be a poet in North Dakota. There is no automatic respect in this square corridor at the faraway top of America for someone who gives his life to poetry. It's regarded as quaint and suggestive of *something else going on there* by the earthy pragmatists of the northern plains. The pragmatists of the plains subscribe to the *compensatory* theory of art, that anyone who veers far from the narrow norm of heartland life is compensating for something that went wrong, like a kid who learned to type with his feet because he has no arms. Such poets as we have either leave or gravitate to the squat towers of the two university English departments on the bank of the Red River, or they publicly disclaim that they love poesy, but shyly concede that they knock out a little cowboy poetry in the winter. On the far side of the Mississippi, certainly on the far side of the Missouri, cowboy poetry alone is regarded as legitimate.

Murphy's biography is a kind of belletristic Paul Bunyan story. He was born in the big blizzard of 1951 in Hibbing,

Minnesota, where his parents, both lovers of literature, were professors at the local junior college. His parents rented a flat above the Zimmerman store in downtown Hibbing. They hired a boy to push wee Tim's stroller. "He sang to me. His name was Bobby Zimmerman, and you know him as Bob Dylan." The great goddess Serendip had a hand in that. Boy Dylan was ten at the time, baby Tim was a newborn. The family moved to Moorhead, Minnesota, six months later. The answer, my friends, is living in the wind.

Murphy attended Yale University from 1968-72. At Yale, Robert Penn Warren was his tutor. On September 5, 1969, the great novelist set the destiny of young Murphy's life. When he learned that Timothy wanted to be a poet but did not know how scansion worked, Warren wrote out Donne's sonnet, *If Poysonous Mineralls*, on the chalkboard and read it through with exaggerated emphasis on the metrics. "Over the course of the next hour I received the only formal training in poetics I ever got. I asked him why he didn't teach courses in poetry. 'Can't be taught. Either you've got it or you don't. You do, but you need to be immersed in verse.'" Warren demanded that Murphy memorize the first 109 lines of *Paradise Lost* before their next meeting. Before their work together ended, Warren had induced Murphy to memorize 30,000 lines of English verse.

Tim Murphy writes mostly in rhyme. Like his beloved Robert Frost, he prefers not to play tennis with the net down. Robert Penn Warren, at Yale, may be said to have raised the net for "a freckled, red-haired eighteen year-old" from Moorhead, Minnesota. And yet Murphy, now 60, freely admits how crazy it is to spend a lifetime writing line after line with rhyme after rhyme. Still, it beats surrendering to the threadbare poetic fashions of our times. "Free verse," says he, "ruled the roost for a hundred years, and it is old, damaged, tired and well nigh unsalvageable." His poetry is mostly spare. I heard an echo of

Eliot's *The Hollow Men* in one of the many poems he recited, but I dared not ask him about it. He's deep in, and yet never inauthentically in, the great tradition. He doesn't write like an English major, but like a poet who has read everything and absorbed some of it and is now working through problems that other poets have worked, but in a faraway improbable place.

When Penn Warren was through with him, he passed Murphy on to Richard Wilbur. "Because he's the best man we've got," Warren told Wilbur. Murphy sent the "the great man . . . a sheaf of my awful poems." And waited. Here's Wilbur's reply, on a note card carefully saved and examined like a koan for more than 30 years. "Dear Mr. Murphy, I get poems over the transom every day, and I never respond to any. In your case I shall make an exception, however. I think that you have a command of the pentameter line and rhyme. I caution you, however, that your using the matter of Constantine Cavafy does not excuse you from the task of sufficiently charging your words." (If you look up Cavafy you will see that Wilbur was saying that paradoxical confessionalism is not, in the end, sufficient).

By now, Murphy has published a significant amount of poetry. But he didn't publish a book until he was 47 years old. He speaks of "my long years of living under a rock on the prairie." That is to hide your poetic talent not under a bushel, but under a rock dragged onto the far southern shore of paleo Lake Aggasiz by a glacier that began its journey up on the Canadian Shield. Murphy is alive to the geography and the geology of North Dakota. He says, in *Missouri Breaks* that the Dakota landscape is "legible as a Bible for the blind." This is partly disingenuous. More than others, Murphy knows how difficult a text the Bible is. He's one of the few Dakotans who really know how to read the text of the land here.

The Deed of Gift was published in 1998. The 26 years between Yale and *The Deed of Gift* might be called the lost decades of Timothy Murphy, lost to drink and capitalism, not that he regrets either. *Set the Ploughshare Deep* was published in 2000, *Very Far North* in 2002, and his translation, with his partner Alan Sullivan, of *Beowulf*, was published in 2004.

His body is a little dried up, as the second decade of the twenty-first century begins, but his Muse is flowing like the sly, magical Wild Rice and the Sheyenne Rivers in the region of North Dakota where he lives. Sometime during our wanderings in the snow I asked Tim if he worries that his muse will fly away with the wind. "I'm writing much better poetry now than I did in my fifties," he said. He made it clear that his creative juices are exfoliating rather than withering, even though he has in many ways lost "my body's long quarrel with my mind."

So far, Murphy is not much known or read in North Dakota. As he said recently, he's better known in Edinburgh, Scotland, than in Edinburg, North Dakota; more recognized in Havana, Cuba, than in Havana, North Dakota. In publishing his poetry, the Dakota Institute Press intends to change that. Just because North Dakotans and the people of the American heartland are not yet much aware of his work, does not mean his work is not much worth knowing. Murphy is a major poet of the English language who has chosen to live among us. The peculiarities of his life, the lost decades, his determination to spend a fair portion of his energies in the insurance business (like Wallace Stevens) and his quixotic tiltings as a Dakota farmer, have kept him away from the academic appointments that pass for an American imprimatur in poetry. But as most Midwesterners have gone about their business oblivious to the major talent in our midst, Murphy has unceremoniously placed his poems in the best poetry journals of the English-speaking world and earned the respect of the major poets of our time. It would be a squandering to let him win acclaim on several continents but not in the near counties of his homeland. We are publishing his poetry for his existing readership, spread across what he calls the Anglophonic world, but also for the people who have yet to discover his voice.

He deserves to be known and celebrated in North Dakota and on the Great Plains. His muse is agrarian. Agrarian, but also deeper than agrarian, as deep as the grass our great, great grandparents plowed in the name of Jeffersonian democracy. (Murphy has a Jefferson poem, but it is about financial profligacy, not Jefferson's impossible vision of a pastoral utopia). Better yet, Murphy's poetry is a confirmation of his hero Frost's view that *the land was ours before we were the land's*. More than California or Colorado or even Connecticut, North Dakota is a platform onto which well-meaning people have transferred a European software, without ever asking how the land would recommend we live on its grassy bosom. And while we squared it off and plowed the living daylights out of it, and exported topsoil and our children in equal heedlessness, quietly at the margins of our hectic conquests stood the Indians, the Mandan, the Hidatsa, the Arikara, the Ojibwe, the Lakota, the Dakota, and the Assiniboine, ready to tell us what they have learned over the millennia. But instead of hearkening to those who were the land's, we whupped them, rounded them up, tucked them out of the way, and relegated them to crossover pow wows and public appropriations of what we take to be tokens of their culture. The lessens we have learned have come in disaster—don't expose all of the dirt in times of drought, don't plant the whole state to wheat when the price is set somewhere else, don't count on your children seeing in this place what you pretend to see in it. We've imported a near eastern religion to a far country, with considerable success, but the dysfunction between the voice of the land, "legible as a Bible for the blind," and the dominionism of the Judeo-Christian tradition, has created some deep identity confusions in the history of the Great

Plains. It is not for nothing that North Dakota has the worst teenage binge drinking problem in the country, and the severest adult alcoholism in America. I think it is certain that the people of North Dakota, like the people of the Great Plains, still possess what they are unpossessed by, still withhold, still bluster and borrow this side of surrender. I don't think even Tim Murphy has figured out how the land can be ours and we the land's within the industrial and Jeffersonian paradigms of our experience. But he's not nearly done writing this place. We need poets to wrestle with the angel of this remote precinct. We have a right to call upon Murphy and some others to take the wound for us.

Murphy is an agrarian, but he is not a nostalgist. He sees the new North Dakota with its gorgeous machinery, GPS-equipped, and much better marketing savvy as the salvation of this place, or at least the means by which the northern plains will continue to have a sufficient economy to support its modest population. When he's not writing verse, he's essentially an agribusinessman, which is not quite what you would expect. He's owned large acreages, made and lost fortunes in farming, and served as a director for a hog confinement factory. He's not exactly agrarian in the yeomanry sense. He doesn't seem to have much money at all, but he is not ashamed to talk about making money. He's different from any poet I have ever met. He's a political conservative. He doesn't wear his politics on his sleeve, but he's not a literature department poetical Marxist, that's for sure.

We had a low-tone conversation about poetry and place, poetry and spirit of place, as we followed skittish pheasants around the sloughs of the Sheyenne River Valley in southeastern North Dakota. Most North Dakotans don't make room in their lives for poetry, I asked. He said, without lament, a people without poetry has no soul. He meant poetry in some bigger way than verse. He's just the kind of poet North Dakotans can find it possible to read. He's one of us. He writes about farming, hunting, the land and the sky, dogs, cattle, shotgun shells, and his recipe for pheasant stew. His poetry is not impossibly abstract or elusive. In fact, it is disarmingly accessible, which may make some think it less sophisticated and accomplished than it is. He's not particularly interested in writing *New Yorker* poetry. He likes the idea that his books might appear in Scheels or Cabela's stores. He has no interest in writing inexplicable poetry.

Tim Murphy is a bundle of identities that he is more candid about than just about anyone I have ever known. He wrote, just yesterday, "I'm essentially a confessional poet." Before you have read more than a handful of the poems in this book, you will know more about Murphy than most people withhold over a lifetime. I think that is his actual genius—self-revelation that is not narcissism, candor that is not the pose of candor, a willingness to look life in the face, even when it's withered, and report what the mirror on the wall speaks. The mantra of good writing is "write what you know." Bad poets don't. Most poets are bad. Murphy writes what he knows—himself, his friends, his lovers, his family, his dogs, his wanderings, his hunts, his longings and lapses and losses—with a stark simplicity that virtually always rings true. You get the sense when you are with him that he doesn't hold back.

We had about six hours together and during that time he composed a couple of poems. In his head, of course, because it was far too cold to be grappling with paper and pen. He's put an enormous amount of wear and tear on his body—shattered it in some ways—but when you are with him you are still mostly struck by his youthfulness—through cigarette-stained teeth. He ceases popping cigarettes into his mouth only often enough to tell you he knows how obnoxious the habit is. I was sitting in the back of the vehicle. His brother was driving. Murphy's dog

Feeney was making a spectacular amount of noise right behind my left ear—whimpering, whining, barking, howling, moaning, muttering—aching to get out on the land and after birds. Murphy said Feeney can keep up that symphony of sounds that do not belong in a closed car for a full 500 miles without pausing to regroup, but the minute the dog has the chance to grip a few pheasants by the neck in an open field somewhere, he settles down and mostly sleeps on the drive home. Whenever Murphy opened the window a crack to let the smoke of his cigarettes burst away, the wind through the window threw me against the back of the back seat, against the yammering Feeney. It was at such moments that Tim would say, "So tell me about your own love of poetry." I could not reply, "sure, once my lips thaw out."

I asked Murphy how long is your dog Feeney likely to live. He gave an equivocal answer but the translation is *a couple more years*. I asked how much he grieves the death of his dogs. More than for humans, he said, but I knew that wasn't quite true. But deeply. His longtime partner Alan Sullivan died on July 9, 2010. In the months that followed Murphy spiraled all the way down. I don't honestly know how he winched himself back to the surface. He was walking ahead of me when I asked my question. He turned, "Our dogs teach us how to die."

In *Cold Front*, Murphy wrote beautifully of his relationship with Alan:

> My love (once such a darling)
> is now a wintry spouse,
> sullen—sometimes snarling—
> because I'm a lying souse,
> because I can't quit tippling
> or spirit us from the snow—
> or be the winsome stripling
> he wooed so long ago.

Murphy has called his poetry "bleak." That's not the overall impression one gets from reading his work. Even when he sees the world through a glass bleakly, as he often does, there is a vitality in his poetry that lifts it out of gloom. The rhyme alone is a kind of optimism. The first of the two collections in this book, *Mortal Stakes*, is, as Murphy tells it in his preface, "the work of some hard years before the drinking nearly killed me on September 14, 2007. It's a pretty black collection of poems, alleviated only by the joy of my hunting and the first glimmerings of hope through faith."

How well the faith, abandoned early, recollected late, will hold up in the long run remains to be seen. Murphy is sufficiently militant about it to prove that this is a drama that is not yet out of the second inning. The Dakota Institute will see the story through. With enormous respect and pride.

Clay S. Jenkinson
Editor-in-Chief
The Dakota Institute Press

PREFACE

Against the typical landscape of today's poetry, the work of Timothy Murphy shines like a torch in a fog. Many a current magazine is clogged with the effusions of blatherskites so longwinded that often you wearily turn a page only to find to your disappointment that the poem you were plowing through hasn't ended after all. But Murphy, to his great credit, is always concise. He is fond of closure--of the kind of poem that (to quote Yeats) ends with a click like a closing box. As his late friend, fellow poet, and collaborator Alan Sullivan remarked, Murphy's poems tend to be "terse as gunshots in duck season." Moreover, he strives to write lucidly, determined to make his poems perfectly comprehensible to all.

Murphy has recalled that Robert Penn Warren, his mentor at Yale, once insisted while pouring him a drink, "Boy, the first line of a poem has to grab you by the throat and say *poetry* the same way this Jack Daniel's grabs your throat and says *whiskey*." The lesson struck home. When we start reading a Murphy poem, its compactness and firm rhythm tell us right away that it isn't prose, making us want to imbibe still more.

A longtime resident of North Dakota and a celebrant of prairie life, Murphy may well be the most outstanding regional poet we have had since Robert Frost. Regional his work may be, but as Anthony Hecht has noted, it isn't provincial at all. "I live surrounded by a desolate beauty," Murphy told an interviewer; "I am in love with the horizontal grandeur of the prairie." In these poems, as in his memoir, *Set the Ploughshare Deep* (2000), Murphy eloquently speaks of that territory and its inhabitants. As farmer, hunter, fisherman, and small-town entrepreneur raising capital for farming and hog-raising, he has known at first hand both the cruelty of the seasons, with their unpredictable storms and floods, and the lavish bounty that, when it so chooses, the fertile prairie can bestow.

During his long post-college years while he was making a living and perfecting his art, Murphy did not hurry into print. At 47 he finally brought together twenty years of work in his first book, *The Deed of Gift* (1998). With that collection he quickly took his place among the leading formalist poets of his time. In 2002 Philip Hoy, London-based editor and publisher of the impressive *Waywiser Press* series, added Murphy's *Very Far North* to his highly selective list.

This new book you hold in your hands, harvesting the work of nine years, proves that Murphy hasn't been standing still. It combines two ample collections, and although either could stand by itself, together they tell a deeply moving personal story. For all the recognizable elements of Murphy's previous poems--prairie landscapes, portraits of cherished people--*Mortal Stakes* introduces an unexpected theme: the poet's finding his way back to God. In "Case Notes," a candid self-history, he reveals what led to his re-conversion; "Cross and Veil," which soon follows, voices a healthy fear of the Last Judgment. Truly felt, well-crafted devotional poems have been rare in recent American letters--offhand, I can think only of Dallas Wiebe's heart-wrenching, "On the Cross" besides--and so Murphy's contributions may seem almost revolutionary. His reconciliation with his faith, won through hard combat against despair, has given us lyrics of depth and power.

> A blooded dog quarters the feral rye,
> and my body's long quarrel with my mind
> is silenced by a landscape and a sky
> legible as a Bible for the blind.

With startling candor, *Faint Thunder* recalls the poet's struggle to recover from alcoholism, to fight his way back to everyday life, sustained by his faith and friendships, by the surrounding North Dakota earth, and (not least) by Feeney, his loyal retriever. The two parts of this book tell of one man's endurance through crises and setbacks, losses and near-disasters. And hearteningly, *Faint Thunder* ends on a positive note: with a prayer for more years "to walk and memorize this land."

Deliberately, like a mason laying stones, Timothy Murphy sets words in place so that they stay put. Not for him is a fashionable critical emphasis on the transitory process of writing; for him, what counts is the final result. Murphy's resounding triumph is that he has survived and endured and devotedly kept writing, and has achieved so many fine poems along the way. As poem after poem will show and as I believe the future will confirm, his works are made to last.

X. J. Kennedy
Lexington, Massachusetts

Mortal Stakes

poems
2002 – 2007

i.m Alan Sullivan

Survivor by Charles Beck

CONTENTS

I. COLD FRONT

II. *SWA HIT AEROR WAES*

III. HUNTER'S LOG

IV. PRAYER FOR SOBRIETY

I. COLD FRONT

Waking at Anchor

The clouds are aqueous
and the bay nacreous,
scarcely a trace of swell.
The sand longs to be shell,
though shell will soon be sand
and fish, walk on the land.

Last Will and Testament

Each will and codicil
made heretofore by me
I cancel. Let this be
at law my binding will.

Assets of every kind
with which I die possessed
pass to my trust and vest
as I long since designed.

Bankers whose funds I drew
in hardship I enjoin:
leave me the single coin
my Ferryman is due.

My brother James, I name
executor, trustee.
From every obligee
I hold him free of blame.
*

* *indicates poem continues on the following page*

My mother I bid goodbye.
I leave her in good hands.
My younger brother stands
straighter by far than I.

Alan, across the river
the poets abide their glade
where I'll embrace the shade
of my foremost forgiver.

Made and declared by free
intent my written word
and signed by me this 3rd
of March, 2003.

Light-Footed Son

With little to lose
but the pike he twirls
and the steel-spiked shoes
in which he birls,

he hazards all
for company scrip,
the dancing hall
and an amber nip.

When logs and stream
cut loose with a roar,
in his mother's dream
he dances ashore.

The Manly Arts

How to run the table
or shoot doubles on cocks,
lead a mare from her stable,
tan the skin of a fox—

how to batten a hatch
and trim a working jib,
light fires without a match,
grill steaks, wearing a bib—

these are tasks that a boy
must master every day
to his sorrow or joy—
even if he is gay.

Father Jack

A diamond willow grew beside a brook,
roots undercut, bending above the bank.
Carefully carved, it made a shepherd's crook
for one who sorrowed at a bully's prank.

He stoked the campfires as his charges slept
and the dreamt bear crept from its forest cave.
Comforting the youngest when they wept,
tousling their heads, he said "A Scout is brave."

Why he renounced his vows no one can say.
Certainly not for leading boys astray.

Bull Rider

I met a boy who rode the rodeo
and took me hunting on his daddy's spread.
He was so quick he made my swing look slow,
and every cock he pointed at fell dead.

Picture a half ton bull bucking a boy
who weighs one forty, who flirts with broken bones
for eight seconds of panic-stricken joy.
Fine looking kid, his buddies called him Jones.

Summers he bummed from town to drowsy town;
he'd mount Black Lightning, Cruel Clementine,
dust himself off. He told me with a frown
"I ain't no Larry Mahan or Phil Lyne."

Figured he'd ranch, maybe, or study law.
Sported the cutest butt I ever saw.

Cross-lashed

A chapel, not a church:
just a clearing in the wood
of aspen, pine and birch,
where a rude altar stood

pegged by a boy's hands;
behind it a birchwood cross
cross-lashed, but neither stands.
They are gone under the moss.

When I quit Wilderness Camp
I rose up from my knees
and left the altar lamp
burning in the trees.

Summits would loom above
the stony trails I trod.
Sex led me to love;
love bound me to God.

To Peder Anders Sulerud

Compasses set at ought plus four
to make Magnetic true,
we paced the uneven forest floor—
my thrcc strides to your two—

then aimed east through a quarter mile
of fresh-cut aspen slash,
breaking our pace to skirt a pile
of deadfall in the gash.

On lashed towers along the shore,
you taught us how to speak
in Morse–mirror or semaphore–
forgotten like my Greek.

Per Sulerud, last night I sank
beside a bonfire's coals.
Woodcraft and your Eagle rank
were boyhood's loftiest goals

on footpaths where your student stood,
hefting his elder's axe.
Diamond willow and ironwood
and brush cover our tracks

through wilds no boy should navigate
without a watchful guide.
The ardors of the young abate,
the obstacles abide.

The Bowline

A young sailor plummeted from a tree.
Stunned as though a spreader had cracked his head,
he lay six months unmoving, nearly dead.
To rouse him from insensibility
a wise doctor gave him a length of rope,
said "Bowline." The rabbit popped up the hole,
and hopped counter-clockwise around the bole.
Prayers had been heard, a mooring made for hope.

Cross and Veil

for Alan Sullivan

I grew up with *Aurora Borealis*—
in Walhalla, North Dakota, "Northern Lights"
that flickered through our noctilucent nights.
One year, past Hudson Bay, I hiked the talus
that spalled with icefalls from Mount Odin's peak
and reached a plaque that read *Le Cercle Arctique*—
a place so bleak, our dome tent seemed a palace.
Grown old, we leave the Antipode unseen—
the Southern Cross beyond the shimmer-screen
mariners named *Aurora Australis*.

Liferaft

At Pentecost the guest was Father Hughes.
"Suppose that cancer spreads incurably
through one from whom you cannot bear to part.

Devoted spouse, can you accept this news
with some measure of equanimity?
Have you the Holy Spirit in your heart?"

What steered me there that day, what made him choose
a homily for my own misery?
A mariner needs a sextant, compass, chart.

Remission

Key Largo. Alan muscles chain and hook;
his first mate shelves a C.S. Forester book,
   and we are under way,
teeth to the wind before the break of day.

No seabird, Fugle has no main to raise,
only twin engines adding to the haze
   from which the spires of Oz
reach skyward to the porpoises' applause.

If I fetch up friendless, confused and frail,
memories of the mornings we set sail—
   passages such as this—
will be what I preserve of earthly bliss.

Nine Bells

God in His mercy gave
the heavens as a clock
to sailors he would save.

Driven by wind and wave,
I steer for Peter's rock
and moor within his nave,

seeking the faith to brave
my first mate in a smock
and sawbones looking grave.

Watercolor

Our pleasure craft is anchored in the lee
of the egrets' red mangrove rookery.
White floats mark baited crab pots off our bow,
and there an aging couple work the sea.
No great blue herons foraging the green
shallows are as essential to this scene
as he, the helmsman; she, poised at the prow,
wielding the boathook, ladening their scow.

Robert Ward

I love the bells of bascule bridges ringing
and old recordings of Caruso singing,
the underwater songs of dolphins pinging,
as does this poet with so fine an ear.
Though deaf from childhood, he has bones to hear
the double bass, imperative and near,
all but forgotten by the loud and shrill
who never find the silence to be still
or make their words kneel and confound their will.

Buoyed Home

The rolling swell
tolls a sinners' bell
that manifests a shoal.

Green and red
flashing far ahead
will guide me to my goal.

I hope to glide
ghosting with the tide
and moor behind the mole.

A nodding nun
wards my shoreward run
but cannot guard my soul.

Conestoga Bark

My mate feathers the spindled wheel
to right our tipsy bark,
luffing to windward as we heel
rail under in the dark.

Where boys are brown and salt air sweet,
seafarers find no rest
but wake aground in the waving wheat
that runs forever west.

Cold Front

For want of oil a moaning
comes from the weathervane—
spindle and socket groaning
as north winds blow again
and send the real geese flying
to Texas or Mexico.
Our brass goose is dying
to join them, but cannot go.

Here firewood is essential
for keeping folks alive.
Where windchill's exponential
only the snowmen thrive.
Someday we'll board a clipper
and catch a Norther bound
south from the Little Dipper
for Virgin Gorda Sound.

My love (once such a darling)
is now a wintry spouse,
sullen—sometimes snarling—
because I'm a lying souse,
because I can't quit tippling
or spirit us from the snow—
or be the winsome stripling
he wooed so long ago.

II. *SWA HIT AEROR WAES*

The Doorman
i.m. Michael Donaghy

You kept your Hopkins hidden in your hat
to pass time when gypsy cabs were weaving.
A matron in whose presence hats came off
spotted the poet you were forced to doff
and whisked you to her gracious East Side flat
  where seven stories up
  Margaret are you grieving
  over Goldengrove unleaving?
her voice was tea poured in a china cup.
She bought you tickets to the 'Y,' that hall
  where Eliot intoned
his Four Quartets, where Frost said Mending Wall,
and Dylan Thomas sang his lines half-stoned.

Busking for the supper on your plate,
  you married Maddy late,
a gypsy wedding rioting in your heart,
that tympanum where all our meters start.
  A frail expatriate,
you wowed the 'Y.' Your patroness returned
to hear firsthand how much her guest had learned.
She watched you springing for the microphone
  to read without a text,
master of pacing, phrasing, pitch and tone.
Pity the poor bastard who went next,
  yet even he is grieving
  your prematurely leaving
a stage so few could ever wholly own.

V.I.P. Lounge

The most exclusive anteroom in Hades
caters to those who wrote well in their eighties:
classical poets, Pindar and Sophocles
exchanging shop talk with Simonides.

Hardy and Frost, Francis and Hope are there.
Scovell, Virginia Hamilton Adair
and Janet Lewis, sharing a pot of tea,
raise their cups, praising Mnemosyne.

The Goddess turns Her back on the elect
to greet a new arrival, Anthony Hecht,
who takes his place among the Greats in Hell.
Would I could live as long or write so well.

Lux et Tenebrae

Kindness to students is a cardinal act
of mercy at which Professor Hecht excelled,
correcting us with dignity and tact
while holding us to standards he upheld.
Fiat lux, the Lord said to the night.
Hecht's answer was 'The Darkness and the Light.'

Near Mainz, his rattled comrades gunning down
women and children under a white flag,
at Flossenberg (the camp downwind from town)
a fetor fit to make a butcher gag
were horrors that returned when he was dreaming.
He told a friend, "For years I woke up screaming."

For all his blessings—an adoring spouse
whom he revered, a modicum of wealth,
the embassies of poets to his house,
a stronger voice despite precarious health—
he made of suffering an art so dark
few soldiers ever better hit the mark.

David

For the slow death of his father,
the near loss of his mother
and swift death of his brother,
I have a friend who suffers.

An innocent in the Garden,
he shouldered every burden
and marched straight out of Eden
when the angel told him "Go."

He cannot hear the Gospel.
Moses and the Epistles
are no aid in his struggles.
He fleeth from the Father.

To me he is a beacon
of decency and reason.
Someday the Lord will beckon,
and David can turn home.

Writ of Attachment

It is my fault, my most egregious fault,
I lived as grandly as a landed lord
while prudent men cached bullion in the vault
where reputation and respect are stored.

Here the accusatory ledger stops:
all the improvidence and blame are mine.
I spent my revenues from dwindling crops
on books and art, a cellar stocked with wine.

The part I've played too grandly is a role
I must unlearn. The Hindoo in his thatched
wayside hut has but a beggar's bowl
to win treasures never to be attached.

Monticello, June, 1826

Words For My Forebear, Perhaps

"Do not despair, love. Do not grieve,
though you're with child and I must go
from a wharf white with snow.
Trust that we take not now our final leave."

"Somewhere I'll find an unclaimed swale,
and there bailiffs who cannot wait
for the maize to ripen late
will never march their tipstaffs down the trail."

"When I have earned your steerage fare,
you and the child can follow me
to where rack rent will be
a bitter memory of County Clare."

Lealty

In a small country graveyard
I watched a man of ninety
crossing himself and kneeling
before a tilted headstone.
I saw he was a farmer
by his Carhartt coverall
and wondered at his stature
unbowed by work or weather.
After he planted flowers
I glanced at the engraving
from Nineteen Twenty-seven
to "Beloved Wife, Maria"
and an infant son, Jason.
The clan name was Chisholm;
their tartan clad my forebears.
What drove them from the Highlands
to our Red River Valley—
hardly a plot in heaven
and half the world from Scotland?
I'll never know their story.

End of the Line

I must be getting old
to think so much of the dead—

not the Great Dead who rolled
hexameters through my head,

but tradesmen who bought and sold
insurance, beer or bread—

the stories my father told
a son who failed to wed.

The Great Moorhead Fire

Joe Kippels ran a department store
outclassed by James Cash Penney,
and old Joe could have torn his hair
except he hadn't any.

Bill Kenney milked the Silver Moon
for seventy cents a pour.
As Main Street filled with smoke one noon,
a drunkard at his door

cried "Kippels' store is burning down!"
Never a man to borrow,
Kenney said with a puzzled frown
"I thought that was tomorrow."

Two Miles West

"Roses and lilies two miles west,"
said the red paint on whitewashed plank
nailed to a burly trunk that sank
like a drover on an ample breast.

Once creaking oxcarts rolled this way
over the wilderness of grass
whose stems whispered 'Alas, alas,'
as the plough cleft the virgin clay.

Where wayworn mothers came to nest
and chain clinked on the swingle ring,
what profit did the flowers bring?
"Roses and lilies two miles west."

Reburial

She sleeps encircled by beans and wheat,
but no fruit tree shades her head,

so I shall transplant a Connell Red
to this grove where rivers meet.

Long may its laden branches wave
and apple falls be sweet

when my father, risen from his grave,
rests at his mother's feet.

Ischemic Event

The mirrors where the mallards come meant sloughs,
and *rooster wagon* was the hunting car
rushing him to the hospital ER.
My backseat labrador was *Drooling Flews*
and a long wingshot, *Father never choke.*
Told of the metaphors by which he spoke
he laughed "At long last I have met my Muse."

Riderless Horses

"Why do we mourn? He lived to eighty-two!"
Soc Glasrud said, tears coursing down his face,
a weathered headland where the decades drew
furrows that death will all too soon erase.

My father's youthful face was disarranged
when a rogue draft horse kicked him in the head.
By words, not blows, we later were estranged
but I forgive a man now four years dead

whose last confession was "I've been too dark,"
whose final, whispered insight was "Vince wins."
Lord, may his knack for words that hit the mark
win him remission of his venial sins.

And when I bear Soc Glasrud to his hearse?
More boots to fill or stirrup in reverse.

Swa Hit Aeror Waes
i.m. Clarence Glasrud

As "weathered headland" I described the face
of a Norse friend crowding ninety-four,
half deaf, and wholly in a state of grace.

At *Hronesnaes* the hungry fulmars soar,
and combers roll shoreward at such a pace.
How do you cry *"Farvel!"* above the roar?

III. HUNTER'S LOG

Missouri Breaks

I am a trespasser on treeless ground,
home to the sharptail and the furtive hun,
and here the tallest thing for miles around
is a small hunter shouldering his gun.

A blooded dog quarters the feral rye,
and my body's long quarrel with my mind
is silenced by a landscape and a sky
legible as a Bible for the blind.

The Great Chain of Eating

Last night I heard the vast mosquito hatch.
Now big brown dragonflies swarm from the wood,
circle above our apple trees and snatch
mosquitos hungering for human blood.
Gorging on dragonflies, the swallows swoop
until the peregrine perceives her prey
darting below. She folds her wings to stoop,
smashing a swallow in a puff of gray.

So in Montana, when I lofted flies,
brookie, brown or cutthroat trout would rise,
fat with the blood of bugs that fed on mine.
I poached my catch beneath a lodgepole pine
and cached my fishbones far, far from the camp
to foil the bears. Then lit my Coleman lamp.

Envy

The cock oriole perches
atop a catkinned limb,
whistling as he searches
for hens to mate with him.

Deep in the woods a veery
puffs up his creamy breast
to serenade his dearie,
outsinging all the rest.

Contestants in our orchard,
ambitious warblers throng,
tiny poets tortured
by one another's song.

Tide Race

The wood duck's wood-pecked house
creaks in an April gust.
A drumming sharptail grouse
dances the grass to dust.

Round-bottomed as a boat
that sails his flooded fen,
whistling an alto note,
the cobb pines for his pen.

Gales rush from the south,
and geese at tailwind speed
seek the Mackenzie's mouth
to be the first to breed—

to stand watch at a nest
in *Nunavut's* Northwest.

Birthday Dog

You are fourteen. Multiply by seven:
your age in human years is ninety-eight.
How long until you couch in canine heaven?
My one-time watchdog snores as children skate
circles outside her many-cushioned house.
Do you remember your two thousand doves,
pheasants and partridge, geese and sharptail grouse?
You were their mistress, they your scented loves—
feathery pillows when the hunt was done—
and I? I was your double-barreled gun.

Perro del Amo

Go where the blue wings flash
over the whitecapped wave,

where crippled mallards splash
and every bitch is brave.

When the returning dove
roosts at your mother's grave,

I'll bury a box of ash
beside her in the sod.

Vaya con Dios, love,
you were the dog of God.

Too Old For This Game

I flushed six roosters from a frozen slough
and knocked one down with barrel number two.
Wingtipped by a Federal .20 shell,
a pheasant cock can always race like hell.
The drift rose cattail-tall in the marsh's lee.
I broke through crust. Chest-deep, I paddled free.
Feeney, gone wild with tracking so much scent,
couldn't imagine where our cripple went.
In knee-high snow we charged most of a mile,
pitting our wind against the rooster's guile;
then, triumphant, I trudged back to the truck
with bird in vest by dint of dog and luck.
I kenneled up my son of a champion bitch,
gutted the cock, and threw up in the ditch.

Long Shot

It flushed wild and swung so far ahead
that turned downwind it didn't look much bigger.
The F150 length by which I led
was perfect for my Parker's full-choke trigger.
The magnum lead haloed around the red,
ring-necked cock to which Bold Fenian sped.

I've had no store-bought meat for thirteen weeks.
In autumn I subsist on what I shoot,
fast-flying roosters armed with spurs and beaks
that Feeney finds and fetches to my boot.
Our pheasant casseroles are much adored.
"Rule the birds of the air," saith the Lord.

Unnatural Selection

From orchard aisles they now traverse
a young doe and a slim spike-buck
observe their fecund mother nurse.
A year ago I watched them suck.

The old doe hobbles across our lane,
trailing her bloody afterbirth.
Two infants wobble in her train—
the latest scourges put on earth

to browse snap-dragons to the roots,
ravage the dogwood by our wall,
feast on newly-grafted shoots,
and feed archers when apples fall.

Ducks Lose, Pheasants Gain

Mudholes I used to wade for wingshot drakes
    pass beneath the plough
or harbor grouse and pheasant cocks that now
    dust-bathe in prairie lakes.
Drought can come on so swiftly, heading wheat
    dries to worthless straw.
What ails this wind-bedeviled land, what flaw
    brings unrelenting heat?
What thirst draws down the wells, unclouds the sky?
To ask is to invite the facile lie.

Salsola Kali

Farmers taught me to see our tumbleweeds
    as wind-driven grain drills
    sowing their hated seeds
in every furrow that the tractor tills.
Russian thistles rolling across our hills:
    they grant the upland bird
    which cannot speak a word
in their defense, the nesting place she needs.

Snowgeese

for Charles Beck

The flock is whorled like a translucent shell
and intricate as the tubing of a horn,
its embouchure, the soft foot of a snail
lighting on sand, except the sand is corn,
chisel ploughed and left to build the soil
from which indebted farmers have been torn.

I catch one note—a wild, wayfaring cry
as snow geese splash into a glacial mere.
Framed by moraines under a nacreous sky,
they echo in the chambers of my ear.
How does an ear rival your artist's eye
that sees what I can only hope to hear?

Hunter's Log

for William Huber

I. The Peacemaker

I reach Oahe via the Grey Goose Road,
crossing the dammed Missouri headed west,
a lawsuit weighing on me like a load
carried too long, from which I long to rest.
An eagle swooping down the gullied slopes
races the Bronco as though Rosebud bound.
There the fulfillment of my partners' hopes
depends upon one hunting friend I've found.

A Rosebud Sioux topping three hundred pounds
and six feet five, Bill fills the barroom door.
One chamber clear, his cannon holds five rounds—
Colonel Sam Colt's persuasive .44.
Showing it off, he tells me with a smirk,
"Always go armed. Fighting is too much work."

Mad Mary's Saloon, Pierre, SD

II. Bronco

You don't look right with all your mud washed off,
your blood-stained rugs shampooed, your shine restored.

No more than I'd sound right without the cough
owed to my smokes and all the booze I've poured.

"Whose wheels are these?" my hunting buddies scoff.
Women are from GM; and men, from Ford.

III. Double

Two flapping roosters are a heart attack
that fells me every time except today.
They flush. I fire. Headshot, they tumble smack
into the swamp where Feeney earns his pay.
A bowl of steak tartare, a bed of down?
Or blue eyes fathoming two eyes of brown.

IV. Each Other's Measure

Suddenly we heard the sound of barking—
the snuffling nose that pheasant hunters prize—
the labrador, quartering, flushing, marking.
I glimpsed the wolfish hunger in your eyes

as Feeney zigzagged through the rows of trees,
kicking out flustered hens on either side.
From the dry switchgrass whispering at my knees
two roosters vaulted skyward, and they died.

For my part I admired your untilled fields,
sunflower stalks, wheat stubble holding snow,
each drop of moisture that a winter yields
hoarded to make your desert seedlings grow.

I judged your farming as you judged my hunting,
and neither fellow found the other wanting.

V. To John Murphy

The flushing rooster is a thrill
greater than any kill
in which we've taken part or ever will

until the hunting boots of God
tamp us under the sod
and all the pheasants that we've missed applaud.

Wagging their tails, our dogs will tell
the other labs in hell,
"They killed in order to have hunted well."

VI. Fourth Time Pays For All

We named him Battlecock—
lord of the fields and fens,
head cock of the walk,
pride of the roosting hens.

As one would stalk a buck
with ten tines on his rack,
we chased him in the muck.
Each time we struck his track

he flushed far from the gun,
crowing as he fled
Bold Fenian on the run
and Murphy wasting lead.

Feeney and I have won.
The Battlecock is dead.

VII. Feeney's Christmas

We sneaked into the corn.
They flushed out at the end,
cocks cackling in their scorn
for man and his best friend.

Trudging back to the Ford
I swung round with an oath
as two young roosters soared
and Lord! I drilled them both.

My puppy's Christmas presents
lay flopping in the ditch,
a brace of fragrant pheasants.
Feeney had struck it rich.

VIII. Season's End

A wingshot pheasant, downed but not undone:
with so much cattail slough for you to scour
your last retrieve lasted for half an hour.

Smoking a cigarette, I breeched my gun,
patient until I saw your rooster cower
cornered and humbled by a higher power.

IX. Return to the Rosebud

Sam Gwynn, that artful chef and sonneteer
    flies north to shoot next year
    and steep our quarry in
his marinade of juniper and gin.

Out hunting we'll hear whines from the pickup box
    as loafing pheasant cocks
    roost in the leafless trees
or strut through wheatgrass curried by the breeze.

"Cry havoc and let slip the dogs of war!"
    Feeney and his friend Thor
    will quarter a ravine,
articulated halves of a machine.

Fragrant as Minnesota conifers,
    the stunted junipers
    men and retrievers walk
will mask the scent of every bird we stalk.

*

Will roosters that we flush in range fall dead,
shot through the heart or head
by poets who, alas,
can hardly hit a heifer in the ass?

Our trophies field-dressed and our charges fed
in Huber's Chevy bed,
the weary will convene,
all thoughts turned to Professor Gwynn's cuisine.

When prairie dogs are rolling up their town
just as the sun goes down
and Mars flares into view,
the zenith will be juniper berry blue.

IV. PRAYER FOR SOBRIETY

Prayer for Sobriety

Solitary confinement with your tears?
If hope and love elude you, live in dread
of what awaits your killer when you're dead:
grief measured in eons, not in years.

Case Notes

for Dr. Richard Kolotkin

3/7/02

Raped at an early age
by older altar boy.
"Damned by the Church to Hell,
never to sire a son,
perhaps man's greatest joy,"
said father in a rage.
Patient was twenty-one.
Handled it pretty well.

3/14/02

Curiously, have learned
patient was Eagle Scout.
Outraged that Scouts have spurned
each camper who is 'out.'
Questioned if taunts endured
are buried? "No, immured."

3/21/02

Allured by verse and drink
when he was just sixteen,
turned to drugs at Yale.
Patient began to think
people would see a 'queen'—
scrawny, friendless, frail—
a 'queer' condemned to fail.

4/1/02

Into a straight town
he brought a sober lover.
"Worked smarter, drank harder
to stock an empty larder,"
wrote poetry, the cover
for grief he cannot drown.

4/9/02

Uneasy with late father,
feared for by his mother,
lover, and younger brother.
Various neuroses,
but no profound psychosis.
Precarious prognosis.

How Shall I Drink?'

When you are sick and drunk,
the ones to whom you lie
are those who love you most,

the ones whose hopes are sunk
by all that you deny,
those who embrace a ghost

'nothing can satisfy.'

Prayer for the Bushmills

Murphy carries a pint uncracked
and hidden at his hip.
He trips in the lane. His backside smacked,
he contemplates his slip.

"Mither o' God, tis been some time
since Ireland had a quake."
He quavers with impromptu rhyme,
"Mark how the streetlamps shake!"

As though he shoulders a brewery keg
he staggers up from the mud,
but something wet runs down his leg.
"Dear God, let it be blood!"

Booker's End
i.m. Booker Noe

Lightning struck a Jim Beam warehouse.
Burning bourbon sluicing seaward,
eighteen thousand bursting barrels,
seven hundred thousand gallons!
flambéed every bass and bullhead
spawned for miles downstream from Bardstown.
Kentucky grieves, not for its fishes.

Dodwells Road

From Charlee's polished table
gaze multitudes of faces
her memory retraces,
the drunken and unstable

Dylan Thomas sobbing
before his last disaster,
daunted by every Master
he was reduced to robbing.

There's liquor in the kitchen
untouched since John Ciardi,
brooding on Yeats and Hardy,
perfected his perdition.

Now Edna Ward's daughter,
fretting that I've grown thinner,
lays out a lavish dinner.
Tonight I'm drinking water.

The Seizure

"It's your last wake-up call,"
Charlee would have said,
"Take care that you don't fall."
But she was four weeks dead
when lightning struck my brain,
and every word I'd slur
was just transient pain
compared to losing her.

Mortal Stakes

Partridge flee to the headland straw
when combines take their final lap.
A vixen leaves a severed paw
to free her foreleg from a trap.

The kildeer, feigning a fractured wing,
would lure me past the gravel flat
where spotted chicks are cowering
as though I were some feral cat.

No strategy of fight or flight
liberates me from instinct's grip.
I crave the whiskey's amber light,
the balm of ice against my lip.

Salmon swimming toward a tarn
fatten a grizzly in the foam.
Racing into its flaming barn,
the white-eyed mare is headed home.

The Reversion

Born to go astray,
I fled the Catholic fold
when I was twelve years old,
a lamb who ran away,
prey to the wolves, the cold.

My shepherd piped me home.
Filing into a pew,
I learned what Caesar knew:
all roads lead to Rome
where wolves are mothers too.

No Turning Back

Pierce the Eye of the Needle
no caravan can pass.
Ride without a saddle
a colt, the foal of an ass.
A potter will leave his treadle,
a mason white with grout
kneel to kiss your sandal,
and all the stones cry out.

Scaring the Parish

Am I too tattered to pray?
I have scuffed the tips of my shoes
and they are beyond polishing.
I have frayed my blue jeans' knees
and they are beyond patching.
And Lord, my disarray?
It comes of so much kneeling.

Dakota Virtues

Out here we still pray at our forebears' graves,
and quilting is esteemed among the arts.
The handshake is a contract in these parts,
and most of us believe that Jesus saves.

The Runner

A frosty dawn: it isn't even seven.
I pass a hooded jogger on the walk.
Father? A sidelong grin, no time for talk.
My priest is on his daily race to heaven.

Father Peter

Good Friday, and the church was draped in black.
He'd borne a massive cross up to the altar.
Despite his slender frame he didn't falter,
and his voice carried forcefully to the back:

"I tell an unwed girl 'Thou shalt not kill,'
and the next morning I anoint the dying.
Our unemployed have hungry infants crying;
our uninsured can't pay the doctor's bill.

Only six months ago I was ordained
to bear you witness and console your loss,
to suffer with each victim on his cross—
tasks for which a priest is called, not trained."

Fearing the chosen of the Lord are few,
I knelt unshriven in the sinners' pew.

To The Chief Musician

"Break the teeth in their mouths, Oh Lord," he cried.

We Christians can no longer pray this way
to Him our mortal sins have crucified,
but at our funerals we often say:

"Where shall I find my refuge and hold fast
except under the shadow of Thy wings
until all my calamities are past?"

So from antiquity King David sings.

To the Dean

I was amazed to see *Batter my heart*
in the breviary of a Catholic priest
  who wages battle with The Beast
    and longs to divine your art.

You make it look so easy, Dr. Donne:
from courtier to prelate in a minute
  timed by the human heartbeats in it,
    a sprint to heaven won.

I am the much indebted legatee
of lines four hundred years have not erased,
  your ardent lover, *never chaste*
    except you ravish me.

God was the sitting judge for your complaint.
Amice curiae, win for me relief
  from mortal sin as though my brief
    were argued by a saint.

To St. Paul on his Feast Day

Reading my congregation your account
of Christ's heavenly light that struck you blind,
I thought God in His mercy seized your mind
and threw one Hell-bent rider from his mount.

Have you no ears to hear nor eyes to see?
Father and Son and Holy Spirit ask us.
Most of us gallop blindly toward Damascus,
goaded by guilt and fleeing Calvary.

Prayer for Sobriety

Morning glories climbing the garden wall
vie with the fragrant jasmine to outshine
the sun emerging from a summer squall.
Blossom and vine, lover and love entwine.
He is the Groom, and I? The shy betrothed
enraptured by the faith I so long loathed.

This is the sacramental cup we drink,
this the unleavened loaf on which we dine,
deliverance from the sins to which I sink.
Here is the book, the work of my Divine
Redeemer at whose Word the worlds revolve.
Let me return His passion with resolve.

NOTES

Bullrider: Larry Mahon and Phil Lyne are in the Rodeo Cowboy Hall of Fame.

The Bowline: Scouts and sailors are taught to tie the bowline by this mnemonic, "The rabbit comes up the hole, round the tree, and back down the hole." The sailor in this poem is Nicholas Robbins, son of the New England poet Deborah Warren.

The Great Moorhead Fire: My father was lunching with Bill Kenney in the Silver Moon the day Kippel's store burned down.

Lux et Tenebrae: 'Light and Shadows' in Latin. Via the Vulgate version of King David's psalm, *tenebrae et lux* becomes 'the darkness and the light' in our King James Bible, providing Hecht with the title for his last collection of poems.

Swa Hit Aeror Waes is Anglo-Saxon for As It Always Was, *Hronesnaesse*, for the Seal's Nose, and *Farvel*, for Farewell.

Tiderace: *Nunavut* is a quasi-autonomous Inuit province, formerly known as the Northwest Territories.

Perro del Amo: Dog of the Master, or Dog of God.

Long Shot: An F150 is a full-sized Ford pickup. It is roughly the length I had to lead this distant, downwind bird.

Salsola Kali: Scientific name for the tumbleweed, a wild amaranth.

Snowgeese: Charlie Beck's woodcut prefaces the second section of my prosimetrum, *Set the Ploughshare Deep*.

Hunter's Log: "Suddenly we hear the sound of barking" and "He kills in order to have hunted well" are found pentameters from Ortega y Gasset's *Meditations on Hunting.*

Booker's End: Master Distiller for Jim Beam and Jim Beam's great-nephew, Booker Noe died soon after the Bardstown calamity, perhaps of a broken heart.

INDEX OF TITLES AND FIRST LINES

FAINT THUNDER

Poems, 2007-2008

I have heard the pigeons of the Seven Woods
Make their faint thunder...

W.B. Yeats

Reçu en rêve

Mon Seigneur, mon Roi,
Sacré-Coeur, ma loi,
j'espère, je crois.

Timothy Murphy

Canvasbacks by Charles Beck

CONTENTS

I. TWO HANDS PRAIRIE

II. IN DAVID'S LINE

III. WIND RIVER JUSTICE

IV. THE CHASE

I. TWO HANDS PRAIRIE

Working Stiffs

I. Benedict Farms

Plagued by the lack of jingle in my purse,
by Keats and Tennyson jingling in my ear,
I double-clutched to ease into reverse.
A ten-year-old showed me his new John Deere.

He taught me PTO, the fourteen gears.
Choke—wasn't that something you did on dates?
Not five feet tall, savvy beyond his years,
he jounced beside me through the barbed wire gates,

then sank the disc with a hydraulic lever
into a half section of golden stubble.
It stretched fencerow to fencerow, stretched forever.
"If a wheel spins, downshift, 'cause you're in trouble."

For him my height was no redeeming factor.
"You go to Yale and you can't drive a tractor?"

II. Sod Stripper

Boys are stripping the cedar from my roof.
They dump debris into their high-walled truck,
lever old nails, counter-sunk, bicep-proof,
shingles married and laid by nip and tuck.

I am no roofer but I nailed one once,
his thigh a beam pinned by an eight-inch spike.
Man is a predator. By night he hunts.
Loner, endure the lure of like for like.

I've mucked potato cesspits, shoveled shit.
My loads were heavy and the bruising, hard.
Manual labor? I was no good at it,
and quit! quit! resodding my pastor's yard.

Buckle and muscle, bend and spade the sod,
prove to the Boss you are the tool of God.

III. *Los Techadores*

I've been adopted by my roofing crew.
I bought pizza and passed around my books,
"Poeta, si!," grandly confirmed. "For you
I've written an English sonnet." Sidelong looks.

They could have thrown a sack over my head,
bloodied my red hair with a wrecking bar,
bludgeoned me in the bush, left me for dead,
black-eyed *jovènes* who have traveled far.

Now they are reading San Juan de la Cruz
in Espaillat's transcendent, fresh translations.
Once more a Bride of Christ is breaking news.
Ours is a courtship of two New World nations.

Now when Feeney and I go strolling by,
El poeta y su perro! the roofers cry.

IV. The Axe Head

My cedar bit was balanced for a boy
who weighed one thirty, stood near five eleven.
Too broad for oak, the right tool to deploy
on pine and aspen, mine was the axe of heaven.

I notched new fencerails for our firing range
and once felled eight white pines in half an hour,
young trees, eight-inchers, thought it rich and strange
to lop and lash them for a signal tower.

To Tenderfeet, I taught compass and map,
then dropped a jack pine on a driven stake,
taught constellations. Not for me the slap
of taut tummies flopping on Bad Axe Lake.

It was the woods, it was the hills for me,
Christ crucified, the spirit in every tree.

Agápē

The night you died, I dreamed you came to camp
to hear confession from an Eagle scout
tortured by forty years of sin and doubt.
You whispered Vespers by a hissing lamp.

Handlers, allowing you to hike with me,
followed us to the Bad Axe waterfront
down a firebreak this camper used to hunt.
Through all I said you suffered silently.

I blamed the authors of my unbelief:
St. Paul, who would have deemed my love obscene,
the Jesuit who raped me as a teen,
the altar boy when I was six, the grief

of a child chucked from Eden, left for dead
by Peter's Church and all the choirs above.
In a thick Polish accent choked with love,
Te Dominus amat was all you said.

Prison Chaplain

for Stuart Longtin

Heavy and grey now, dressed in deacon's robes—
I see you in your Speedo at Floyd Lake,
its nylon clinging to those golden globes
you exercised for Moorhead football's sake.

We hiked the Black Trail to Itasca Park,
but now I see a deacon hard at work
explicating the Gospel of St. Mark,
our high school quarterback become a clerk—

in the high sense. A boy with such good looks,
you could have run to Hollywood and whored
but turned to mastery of sacred books
and the manly mimesis of our Lord.

Lifesaver, that was your job at Wilderness,
teaching tenderfoot farm boys how to swim.
Soulsaver, I would call you now and bless
any man who preaches Saint Mark to Tim.

We take our coffee outside for the view,
patrol the walk-about with twelve-foot mesh
where drunks can smoke. What has become of Stu?
The Word. Not on the page but in the flesh.

Prairie St. John's Hospital

"Arise."

The stitches near his chin,
the wrong part of his neck,
a bad jab by a wreck:
the boy so tall, so thin,

not knowing when to kneel,
not knowing where to thrust
the knife, no one to trust,
no house in which to heal.

I'm sober here today
where I've been drunk before,
where staff lock every door
and children stay away.

I'm called here by a dove
to say the word Christ said
to Lazarus, four days dead
and waiting for God's love.

Prairie St. John's Chapel

Hospital Chaplain

to Father Jose Mundadan

I failed you once, the Adolescent Floor,
where those who die, who knows if they are missed?
How often have the children there been kissed?
That was no place for one with no degree
in medicine or in psychology.
Nurses, big women, warded every door.
Bandages were on every other wrist.

Four Poems for Rhina Espaillat

I. Some Assembly Required

If you want bluebirds, first you have to make
a proper house. Start with six scraps of shake,
unpainted cedar shingles, blizzard-worn,
torn from the hiproof of your windfall barn.
Slant-saw the sides to make the ceiling vaulted.
(Here in Montana big skies are exalted.)
Then drill a door hole too snug for a flicker
to burgle when your famished fledglings bicker.
Now choose a meadow with a montane view.
For camouflage, its flowers should be blue.

II. Red State Reveille

Daybreak. A youth at Fargo's Jiffy Lube
reloads his grease gun with an oil-stained tube,
prints out the service records on my truck,
changes three filters fouled with gunk or muck,
rotates the tires and drains the filthy oil,
tops up my fluids. Happy with his toil,
grinning broadly, he sends me on my way
in time for Mass. God bless the USA.

III. *Agnóstica*

"Is it harder to pray in rhyme or rhyme in prayer?"
asked a great lady, who led me up a stair
to a tall tower, climbed by John of the Cross,
who succored my dear Latina through every loss
which might have cast her soul into despair.
And who were there? Christ, John of the Cross,
a lady who prayed in rhyme and rhymed in prayer.

IV. Mock Opera

A master-singer perches in Rhina's elm
much as the Dutchman dominates the helm
of a doomed ship in Wagner's stormy score.

His crew provide him leitmotifs galore.
He soars through warbler, finch, and oriole,
silencing every treetop, gable, pole.

Braving a cross-wind on his tossing limb,
he segues to robin for a choral hymn,
taking the parts of every thrush he's heard.

A hush descends on garden, man, and bird.
With shears in hand, I snip a climbing tea
and toss three stolen roses at his tree.

Farm Boy, Call Kayla

Brady, you went to school with pretty Kayla.
You're six feet one. You're soft spoken and handsome,
and you still haven't dragged her out to dinner?
Rich girl? Easy to marry as a poor girl—
words wasted on this poet by his father.
I chickened out on marrying a woman
skittish as any mallard hen at sunrise.
Ran off. Brady, I am no friend to weddings,
but lines? I've written you this baker's dozen,
telling you to watch out for Kayla's mother
whose real wealth is the merit of her marriage.
All of us know how hard seed is to come by,
and land, harder to come by than a planter.

Mission Church

I dream that you set forth for Buffalo
just as the blizzard winds begin to blow.
A patch of black ice and a crosswind pitch
your little Chevy nosedown in the ditch.
The nearest farm is only half a mile,
but you lie down half way, to sleep a while.

When the day yawns, you waken stiff but warm,
unscathed by that ferocity of storm
whose windchills fell to fifty-five below.
The cornice where you curled, waiting your tow?
No ninth circle prey to traitorous weather—
that snowflake on your cassock? Gabriel's feather.

High Above Oahe

Harry landed his plane,
saw how the farm land slopes,
then piped the lake when rain
failed on those twenty miles
of squared farm he could water,
calves fattened for slaughter.
The law frustrates hopes
but not a rancher's wiles.
Pipes that were doomed to rust,
the dithering engineers,
lenders he'd come to trust—
a herd of milling steers.

John Hancock called me in.
What was their debtor's sin,
the Army Corps, the drought,
corn to be burned for fuel?
I've been to Harry's school,
and I long since bowed out.
My friend's only crime
was running out of time.
Look where his grain bins tower.
A banker's feeble mind
can't apprehend the power
that steers geese to a blind.

People don't understand
the scale on which we farm.
Asked where food comes from, kids
will say "The grocery store."
No, children, from the land
on which a gambler bids
his balls against the storm.
It is a winnowed floor,
this granary we've manned,
often to our despair.
Watch Harry climb a stair.
Man was not made to soar.

Flight to Murdo

for Father Lance Oser

He fled the flooding Red
which choked on ice and snow,
and how far did he go?
To a Best Western bed
four hundred miles away,
two thousand feet higher.
God knows, were he a flyer,
he would go there each day
just as the winter wheat
reclaims its tint of green—
a change of heart, of scene,
a refuge, a retreat.

He saw ten thousand geese
staging, the roadside pheasants.
Then begged a prairie presence,
"Grant that our birds increase."
He glassed a rolling reach
of cows that tourists pass.
Calf frisking in the grass,
he was renewed, but speech?
Let me just say the slope
of grassland where he parked,
each pasture that he marked
was crazed by antelope.

The West

I. Front Range

Lean men prone to heroic understatement,
they have a drawled, laconic way of speaking.
They know that for their debts there's no abatement
nor boundaries to the vistas they are seeking.

No, there's only the Front Range of the Rockies
behind which the westering sun is setting
on stallion breakers too strong to be jockeys
and water rights the Judge of all is vetting.

II. *Jornada del Muerto*

There is one writer I'll re-read this fall
to whom I owe a debt I can't repay,
McMurtry, the creator of Captain Call,
Texas Ranger, and Captain Gus McCrae.

His Brokeback Mountain script, his Lonesome Dove
send me abseiling down a sandstone wall,
boots over rock. Tim and his boyhood love
years back blazed trail for Ledger and Gyllenhall.

III. Winter Wheat

Our prairie views are skewed forever West;
ours is a land of drought and blowing sand,
and any questing eagle can attest
that one must soar to fathom western land.
The sun subsides behind the mountain's chest,
embittered ranchers hoard the Kruggerand,
and last night when I lay down to my rest,
I heard my Father's clarion command:

The word made flesh. I breathed this to Saint John
who stood beside my bride, my own son's cross.
I built you mountains you could climb upon,
and once I even flooded inland seas
where winter wheat now rises to your knees.
You are my child. Do not compound my loss.

Prayer for a Horseman

Thrown from a horse when I was nine or ten,
    (I can't remember when),
    I cracked my head on rock,
was knocked unconscious, and I woke in shock.
Ever thereafter, Father, I feared the horse
you mastered with a minimum of force.

    Instead I mastered dogs,
quartering them on hard, arduous slogs
    through cattail, cane and rush,
urging them forth to fetch the prey they flush,
    posting you in the sun
while dogs and boys worked pheasants to your gun.

I came to fear your anger in old age
    which whiskey turned to rage.
Husbandry, horseman, it was your way of life.
    Though I have wed no wife
and sired no sons, no daughters with red hair,
Murphy I sign, and sign with cross and prayer.

Two Hands Prairie

Dream of the Great Plains as a pair of hands,
and every finger is a lengthy river.
South hand points northward, and the north hand south.
The Horse Culture with all its rival bands
endured whirlwinds, blizzards, pox and drought.
The bow lies broken by a beaded quiver.

Rainy River, the Red Deer, and the Red,
Souris, Saskatchewan, all form the Nelson.
Flowing forever north, all of them bend
over a land where hopeful youngsters wed
and send their sons somewhere afar to soldier.
Two hands extend in friendship toward a border
which neither nation's army need defend.

Hand reaching north, the Arkansas, Ohio,
Missouri, tributaries in their dozens,
El Río de las Ánimas Perdidas
en Purgatorio, in Colorado,
and the Belle Fourche, forking into the Powder—
rivers, like men, have many distant cousins.

II. IN DAVID'S LINE

In David's Line

I've no faith in the power of my prayer.
Grant me the grace to phrase
a song of thanks and praise
from one who lists among his sins despair.

Ash Wednesday

Joel 2:13-14

In King James Joel asks "Will God repent?"
Modern Bibles tell us the prophet meant
God will "relent" when we are penitent.
I ask a Hebrew scholar for a hint,
crosscheck the Vulgate and the Septuagint.
Metanoia: a change of heart for Lent:
mischievously I ask "Will God repent?"

The Seven

Acedia

A lassitude, mistranslated as Sloth
      by men who wore the cloth,
Acedia is very near despair.
Call it the precondition for a prayer.

Avaritia

For thirty years I schemed to strike it rich,
but I was a false lover, rightly spurned
by *Avaritia,* that greedy bitch.
Hers were not the riches for which I burned.

Invidia

"Desiring this man's art and that man's scope"?
When in despair with Sonnet Twenty-nine
      I all alone repine,
Dante tells me I'm damned. "Abandon hope."

Gula

Aquinas clad in flab—
punishment for a sin
which I am innocent of.
Distance runner thin,
I was no muscled slab—
no Greek with olive skin—
when mastered by the love
where all my dreams begin.

"Such gluttony!" I cry.
But drink? I am unmanned.
Pour me a shot of rye
and still my trembling hand.

Superbia

Pride is the face I put on shame,
   the arrogant refulgence
for which the Lord will strike my name
   from the book of His indulgence.

Luxuria et Ira

What a long way to climb,
bearing so large a load.
Diminishing, the time
left to me is my goad.
Is time itself the climb?

Lust has left me behind.
Cached alongside the road,
all that a juvenile mind
dreamt that his loins were owed
I leave buried behind.

Staff, keep to the path.
I throw away my dear
anger, rising to wrath,
native to me as fear.
Feet, keep to the path.

To Timothy

Bring me my cloak. Bring Mark.
This prison cell is dark
and Luke, my only friend.
I am very near the end,
nothing much left but bone.
The shackled mastiffs bark,
and other prisoners groan.
Mortal this cold, this dark.
Bring me my cloak. Bring Mark
whom I can lean upon.
And if you find him, John.

Prière: pour deux, mon Dieu

Prayers for the dead crowd out prayers for the living.
Few that I've loved died in a state of grace,
penitent and anointed. All-forgiving
Father, let two of them behold Your face,
masters, mentors, for whom I say thanksgiving.

There is no balm in Gilead or liquor.
Blinded and driven down a seawall stair,
Robinson worshiped flame, Lord, not its flicker.
Housman, hanged for the color of his hair,
should hear no footman hold his coat and snicker.

Poets. We are addicted to vainglory.
We dread that we will live our honors out
but yearn to tell Your angels such a story,
all rise in piteous wrath and swell the rout
of those who mourn the sin of Richard Cory.

Tomàs Ò Ciaragàin

To my friend, Magna Carta is breaking news.
Cattle are herded past his burning trenches,
warriors with golden harps and massive thews
pen in their wicker baskets wicked wenches,
our flutes are wretched reeds, our pipes are scrannel,
and Patrick's currach crosses a Celtic channel.

Cruach Padraic

There is a seam of gold
glittering at its thighs.
The mayors of Mayo told
miners to their surprise:
"The gold is good where it lies."

Psalm 8

To the Chief Musician, upon the harp of Gath
A Psalm of David

My Lord, my God—
How excellent is your name on earth,
your glory set above the heavens!
In the mouths of infants, suckling babes,
you ordain the strength to silence your foe,
the enemy who would avenge himself.
The heavens are the work of your fingers
that made the moon, established the stars;
but what is man that you bear him in mind
or the son of man, that you seek him out?
So little lower than the gods,
him you crown with glory and honor
and grant to his rule the works of your hands.
Earth you have placed beneath his feet:
sheep and oxen, beasts of the field,
fowls of the sky, and fish of the sea
passing through the paths of the sea.
Lord, how excellent is your name!

Confessiones 10.27.38

Wrongly believing beauty lay without,
  blindly I flailed about.
  How late did I begin
to realize your beauty lay within.
  To one deprived of sight
  you said *Let there be light,*
  and to my deafened ear
you called, you cried! hoping that I might hear.
  I thirsted, hungered, yearned.
  You touched me, and I burned.
  How late I came to you,
Beauty ever ancient, ever new.
  How late I came to you.

—after St. Augustine

Soul of the North

Out of the wilds, I pray.
Bound by my northern birth
to fish, to hunt the earth
and follow my forebears' way,
I mutter *I have sinned,*
wander the knee-high grass,
flourish awhile and pass
whistling into the wind.

As char swim to the clear
tundra rivers that run
under the midnight sun,
as wolves follow the deer
drawn from ford to ford,
as clamorous geese in V's
throng to the thawing seas—
all creatures of one accord—
my soul thirsts for the Lord.

III. WIND RIVER JUSTICE

The Manuscript

Lines written so long ago:
When will our quarrels cease?
Which one of us will know
grief and the other, peace?

Classmate

"I fear that you are in the gravest danger."

—Francis Xavier McCarthy

I would have splashed my brains against the wall
seconds later, had it not been for your call,
and the world could have washed its hands of Tim
and jettisoned his verse, most of it grim.
Now you confess that *you* have grown depressed?
Fly to Fargo, I'll clasp you to my breast,
such at it is, and with a healing kiss
whisper what I have learned of mortal bliss.

Two thousand miles and forty years away
I hear your manic laughter as I pray,
"Defend my friend from Satan's fatal charms.
Lady, enfold him in your blue-robed arms."

The Lady and the Greyhound
i.m. Charlee

Marshalled, tethered and starved out of its mind,
her last greyhound came from a racing track
where whips raised weals on every bony back
of blinkered hounds, that bursting from a blind
gate at a gunshot, chased to the attack.

Fearful at first, the dog became a friend
accustomed to her friendly discipline,
an ear scratch or a hand beneath the chin,
but spooked, frightened by shadows to the end.
What was could not erase what might have been.

The Ladies at Kent Island

for Mary Meriam

The general and the major
arrive to unveil their boat,
a thirty-eight foot trawler
immaculately afloat.

The aft-deck fills with flowers,
and here is the pot of tea
to welcome harbor strollers,
even my love and me.

The general and the major
discern that we are coupled,
a state like buried treasure
no martial court has troubled.

The aging lady general
throttles her little ship.
The major warps the trawler
out of its slender slip.

They'll cruise now to the ocean.
There the Atlantic swell,
making its blue commotion,
asserts "Don't ask. Don't tell."

Ad Te Domine

Two sailors in a tiderace,
my brother poet and me,
our schooner slewing sideways
to an outrageous sea:
Profundis! I could scream.
What does unfathomed mean?

"No bottom with this line."
Balancing at the chains,
whose arms sufficed to throw
five hundred feet of line
five hundred feet below?
This verse is what remains
of an unfathomed dream.

Disenchantment Bay

for Alan Sullivan

Touch and go. Our Cessna bumped the sand,
    thumped its tundra tires,
    lifted as if on wires,
banked over ice and rocked its wings to land.

We pitched our camp hard by the Hubbard's face,
    some sixty fathoms tall,
    a seven-mile-long wall
seven leagues from Yakutat, our base.

Crack! A blue serac tottered and gave.
    Stunned at the water' edge,
    we fled our vantage ledge
like oystercatchers skittering from a wave.

Now separation has become my fear.
    What was does not console,
    what is, is past control—
the disembodiment that looms so near.

*

Detachment? So an ice cliff by the sea
    calves with a seismic crash
    of bergy bits and brash,
choking a waterway with its debris.

We clear the neap tide beach of glacial wrack,
    pace and mark the ground,
    then wave the Cessna round.
Pilot, we bank on you to bear us back.

Wind River Justice

Alan riding his first horse from Big Sandy
to celebrate his thirty-seventh birthday:
his mare reared in the lodgepoles when a spruce grouse
flushed and nearly pitched him down a switchback.
My own gelding stampeded through a meadow,
and our young wrangler called those ponies "gentled."

We braved Pyramid's boulders, Barnard's clinkers,
apogees of our climbs in the Wind Rivers,
then turned our backs forever on those summits,
Gannet, the tallest peak in all Wyoming,
the Highline Trail cleavered between the Temples.
We limped, blistered, back to our dusty Bronco.

There stood a girl, sobbing beside the stables.
The boy, his terror turned to helpless fury,
and a young ranger argued mixed-use forest,
treeline grazing, lamb-eating bears and coyotes,
leash law and the permitted use of rifles.
Read the rules posted at every entrance.

*

Two hikers had surprised the sheep at twilight,
young *Lykos* growled, then raced across a meadow
three thousand feet above Big Sandy Trailhead,
and a Basque herder shot the German shepherd
which met no blue heeler or border collie,
no, only a rifle. Wind River Justice.

Bernie Kelly sadly saddled his horses.
Bearers rode up, and *Lykos* down the mountain,
but who descends it twenty-three years later,
no longer carrying Murphy or a backpack?
Slippery the scree, the pool below unfathomed.
Where is the meadow and the watchful shepherd?

August 14, 2008

The Reading

Some owlets eye me from a scrub oak tree.
They're fledged and glass me with their yellow eyes,
and not a one will fly off in surprise,
their wing tips rounded, flying silently,
because I bear a gun, because I'm me.

These are Bob Clawson's kids in Acton, Mass.,
and they are unpersuadable by Frost,
their fathers absent and their bearings lost,
and God excuses kids like these from class.
What shall I say to owlets as I pass?

We have our generations, and the gulf
one cannot pass, especially those not fathers.
Childless, I'm here to bless my little brothers
and read to teenage boys the Beowulf.

Aaron Poochigian

"Today, professor, I have prepared the odes."
Here is a youth who eyes the gods' abodes
longingly, Helicon and Parnassus,
who studies Latin from the times of Crassus.
His adolescent pimples disappear,
his stutter too. Without a trace of fear
he belts out Kubla Khan and Dover Beach,
all the Romantic odes I'd planned to teach.
A thousand lines, I hear out every tale,
odes to the west wind and the nightingale,
to evening, intimations, a Grecian urn.
He's brought no book, only his heart to burn.
And there I stand thirty-five years ago
saying those lines to Warren in the snow.

Three Kites

A twelve-foot fuschia feather
trails from the fighting kite.
Twenty pound test, the tether.
It longs to sail all night.

Two makeshift tails, our neckties,
silkscreens of the Immortal
Poets in Paradise,
assault the Western Portal,

borne aloft by a bird
of ripstop nylon stitched
by secret spells, the Word.
Onlookers are bewitched.

Fighter lashed to his wrist,
skybird leashed at his calf,
he flings up from his fist
the fractal kite. His laugh

lifts to the Easter sun.
Cancer, can you be glad?
Three kites dance as one,
and life longs to be had.

IV. THE CHASE

Hunter's Grace

For the crops in our fields,
the cocks in our crops,
good dogs, straight shooting,
we thank thee, great God.

Ecce Canis

From the first slough some forty birds flushed wild.
  Maddened by pheasant scent,
  Bold Fenian was with child
while I triangulated where they went.

North to the mallards' frozen mating hole,
  a second cattail slough
  rimming a bullrush bowl,
we hunted, panting as the pheasants flew,

all but their patriarch who fell stone dead.
  I watched his grandson go,
  a gutshot cock that sped
to switchgrass tufted in the distant snow.

Under those drifts our harder hunt began.
  Eluding every cast,
  it burrowed, bolted, ran
until at last Fenian pinned it fast.

I floundered to a roadside willow stand,
  collapsing on a log
  where Feeney licked my hand.
Unworthy man, behold thy hunting dog.

Huntress

for Dan Treat, DVM

Her first bird was a crippled mourning dove.
She somersaulted down a ditch
head over heels in love,
buttoned her bird and bounded up the pitch.

Her first drake dropped beyond a refuge sign.
Wriggling under the lowest wire,
she swam a perfect line
as though posting a proof of her desire.

Her first goose gave her nose a nasty peck.
Battered by its unbroken wing
she leapt to grab its neck
and growling, dragged it back for me to wring.

Her first loss was her superhuman ear.
Hand-signalled on each unmarked run,
she could no longer hear
whistling wingtips; even at last, the gun.

At fourteen she was walking into walls,
fouling the carpet, losing teeth.
Farewell to mallard calls
and decoy spreads, wild roosters on the heath.

To St. Francis of Fargo fell the chore,
the Nembutol a gentle thrust
to launch her from our shore.
The last look in her fearless eye was trust.

Night Flight

Downward to darkness on my muffled wings
I hunt the wintry silence of a dream
whose spell is shredded by a rabbit's scream,
the coldest, purest note creation sings.
Femur and fur strewn at a supper's end:
bon appetit, Reynard, rival and friend.

Fieldmice and frantic voles submit to law
whose statutes I administer in sleep,
ruling my fields and barnyard by the deep
authority vested in beak and claw.
Focussing yellow irises, I prowl
in the infrared spectrum of the owl.

Checklist

Cheetos and chocolate chips for Tim to nibble,
a shrinkwrapped pound of Jimmy's jerkied deer,
a sixpack of nonalcoholic beer,
for Feneey's sake a Ziplock bag of kibble,

my Thompson .410 pistol underneath
the driver's seat; towrope and jumper cables,
the Game and Fish sunrise and sunset tables,
my lockback Buck knife in its buckskin sheath,

Nitro Solvent, Rem Oil and cleaning rod,
boxes of Super X non-toxic shot—
can there be anything that I forgot?
The truck is packed. The luck I leave to God.

Three Seasons

Feeney the fragrant—
his black coat browned by pond scum,
reeking of birdblood.

My rubber kneeboots
shedding mud in the closet,
cocklebur heaven!

My thirsty Bronco—
choking on pheasant feathers
late in November.

Forty some roosters
cleaned and bagged in the freezer?
Good until Easter.

February 18, 2009

There was a bitch in heat
half a mile west of me,
so Feeney hit the street.
Two stocking caps with curls
ran when they saw him go
but foundered in the snow.

Feeney adores small girls,
such fun to knock them down
or chase them up a tree.
But Feeney is a clown,
and when they pet, he twirls,
proving his canine wit.
Friendships have come of it.

Missing Mass

He hath put a new song in my mouth.
Psalm 40:3

Going to church afield
I bear the Decalogue
as St. Michael, his shield.
My faithful altar dog
precedes me up the aisle,
mile after dusty mile.

A gale sweeps through the choir
and dries the prostrate grass
lightning and prairie fire
forge to beaten brass.
Tinted anew each day,
the dome is blue or gray.

The blood of every bird
I sacrifice this fall
let me translate to Word,
responses to the call
that asks us to record
a new song to the Lord.

Cole

Cole is now six feet three.
So small, slender was he,
his unshaven cheek so tender,
I gave him a girl's gun,
a thirteen one-eighth pull
fitting his winter wool.
Most every shot rang true.
Down dropped the mallard drake,
down wailed the wingshot gander
Feeney plucked from the lake.
I gave him a grade four gun
left by father to son,
in hopes I'd produce my own;
I gave him a Buck sheath knife
and an old Arkansas stone
on which a kid could hone
the dull sides of his life.
A blond, blue-eyed boy,
stockpad fitted to shoulder,
he hadn't far to travel
to gain his mastery
of stubble, slough or tree,
just a few miles of gravel,
a few years to grow older.

Posted

Drive with caution. This township strip of gravel
is much impeded by a herd of pheasants
flaunting their adolescence,
and it is posted thus: Restricted Travel.

Beside me is an unmowed stretch of meadow
Feeney and I were tempted by all summer.
One month hence some Hummer
will cast over this grass its massive shadow

as herds of Fargo bankers, lawyers, brokers,
who have shelled out their seven hundred dollars
on GPS collars
which pointers wear like diamond-studded chokers,

hunt on this land I once farmed to perdition.
God bless the rich. I was one and I know 'em
and say to them this poem
without a hint of malice or sedition:

Feeney and I shall walk and flush some pheasants,
strolling without our double-barreled Browning,
the one of us not clowning
awed in September by an August presence.

The Brummond Quarter

I.

Into the wind and frosted grass we quartered.
So many hens were roosting on that prairie,
that Bricks for Brains (both of his ears were mortared)
raced at a pace no whistle blast could vary
until we reached a slope of silverberry.

A rooster Feeney missed leapt up behind me.
It fell, leaving behind a cloud of feathers.
Sunrise doing its level best to blind me,
I watched my lab coursing through canes and heathers,
waving his black flag high above his withers.

Chasing it down, he fetched it to his master,
who sat high on a hillside, smoking, panting.
This hunt which started out such a disaster,
dog run amock, a hunter raving, ranting,
was now a blessing, leaving nothing wanting.

II.

Minutes later I stood beside my truck.
Afield, Steve told me that he'd had no luck,
only some merry points on flushing hens.
But then I watched him whip round in the fens,
zigzag behind his dogs into the wind
and pound the pterodactyl they had pinned.
Unvested, it was the largest bird I'd seen
since the first cock I missed at age thirteen.

III.

Crippled by an inflamed Achilles' heel,
I've wrong-footed the plowing. So I kneel,
pry off my boot, massage my tortured foot
much as an oak would bend to mend its root.
When Steve returns, with nary a sight of cock,
from flushing hens after his three mile walk,
I limp into the canebreak, tall rice grass
that lures descending pheasants as they pass.
A loafing lurker leaps up from the cane.
Twisting my right foot in my whimpered pain,
I break the rooster's right leg with my gun.
Into the swamp Steve and his bitches run,
another flush. Death at the second shot.
The swamp monster? No longer is, but not,
cornered in cattails, blasted from the air,
gutted, quartered, diced for the gumbo pot.
Tag-teamed. Three dogs, two men. Death isn't fair.

Georgic

for Bryan Stotts, District Ranger

This is the shoreline of a glacial lakebed.
Some of its flora, fauna are endangered.
Not so the leafy spurge, vile interloper,
the milkweed strewing cotton to the breezes.
Not so the cottonwoods or dwarfish scrub oaks,
the white-tail deer that multiply like chipmunks.
Here autumn daubs its trees above the stockponds
by fours or fives. We have no soaring forests,
just refuge for the wild, pinnated chickens
on a last vestige of the tall grass prairie,
a gift the cattle graze and take as granted.

Feeney flushes a frantic, dustpan dancer
from silverberry bushes in these sandhills,
the blown dunes of the Sheyenne National Grassland
where so much rain has fallen this October,
that tall grasses binding erosive hillsides
are succulent and seeding out of season.
In a damp oxbow looping by the Sheyenne
I once dug up a white-fringed prairie orchid,
fragrant by night, pollinated by sphynx moth
or butterfly, the rare Dakota skipper.
Potted it for my mom. It promptly perished.

Spare this land my trowel and the ploughshare.
Broken for barley in the Nineteen Twenties,
a decade later much of it was moonscape,
now colonized by stands of quaking aspens,
each of those clumps a single organism.
Feeney and I shall trace our tracks come April
when the pooled hollows trill with hatching peepers,
when ferns unfurl their fronds in every gully,
grasses and forbs turn sunshine into fodder,
when calves that boys can sling over their shoulders
nuzzle the udders of their mooing mothers.

Rhymes from the Rosebud

I only hold this land in trust.

—William Huber

My bones are those of a deer
frightened by fang and claw,
but you are built like the bear
who downs a longhorn steer
with one swipe of his paw,
and you could devour me raw.

Cottonwoods by the creeks
and scrub oaks in the draws,
cedars the mule deer seeks,
wild plum the rooster claws:
only ten years ago
I stumbled on your land.
I've hunted it in snow,
winds I could just withstand.

From miles away I'd know
your bin site on this ridge.
Twelve thousand years ago
your forebears crossed a bridge
where now the Bering Sea
pummels a Russian shore.
Dream of those rocks with me.

William, I have learned more
of *heartbeat* in the hunt
here than I've learned at home,
as has my barking runt.
Down Collins Creek I roam,
learning not just the land
where deer and water flow,
but from the mind and hand
of him who keeps it so.

Fin de saison

This is our second blizzard in six days.
Last night the sun sank through a high cloud haze
just as a rooster tried to run the road.
I jammed in a double copper-plated load,
leapt from the hand-braked Ford still on the go.

Feeney lunged through the ditch to drifted grass,
quartering faster with each zigzag pass.
Eighty yards distant in that 'sessile hush',
I glimpsed a fleck of red, a busted flush
and a black gymnast blasting from the snow.

A flightless cripple armed with razor spurs
grimly gripped in his jaws, four cockleburs
pinned to his shoulder like a *croix de guerre,*
Feeney returned with a triumphant air,
his season finished. Let the blizzards blow.

The Blind Retrieve

for Steve Syrdal

I. Training

He won his ribbon. Last night as it grew dark
I fired the launcher dummy into stubble.
He strained and barked but made a perfect mark,
taking his flawless line. Then ran a double.

He whirled and stopped dead on a whistle blast,
knowing his third, last trial was the blind.
He charged dead downwind on Steve's signaled cast
as if he knew by heart the handler's mind.

Grimly, I ran a quarter mile this morning
with Feeney grinning ear to ear beside me,
lolling beside the slow man he was scorning.
Ingrate, had *he* the stature to deride me?

Eight years ago, his wobbly legs were rubber,
hopelessly short. No muscle to his hinders,
he was a butter tub of puppy blubber.
And mark? Mark? He should have been wearing blinders.

Feeney, we'll run for half a mile tomorrow.
The doves, yes! The Canadian doves are coming
whom you'll retrieve from every fallow furrow.
And grouse? The shortgrass, sharptail cocks are drumming.

II. Scotch Triple

Feeney was loping with a dove in jaw
just as I downed three birds with double barrels.
Then it was Dead Bird, Back! Lay down the law,
and put to rest all of our summer's quarrels.
We were in acorns, like a pair of squirrels.

III. Challenge

Challenge: gunner has four doves on the ground,
dog driven crazy by explosive sound
and glimpse of carnage raining from the air.
Double a pair. Reload. A second pair,
breathe while a birdless sky grants a reprieve.
Sunflowers, worse than corn. The blind retrieve.

IV. Blow Sand Theatrics

Feeney, why are you limping on three legs,
sadly stumbling, a woeful clown who begs
sympathy from your audience of one?
Give me that paw while I lay down my gun.
Lie down, down, down! Don't bite, you little bastard!
Roll over, don't you know you're over-mastered?

Poor cripple, you've been lured by wicked doves
to Mexican sand burrs, and I have no gloves,
no pliers. Love, were I a few years older,
I couldn't hoist you on my scrawny shoulder
and, to your Canis Minor, play Orion,
though once I played Androcles to a lion.

V. Drain Eleven

Mournful beside Cass County Drain Eleven,
two fathers with two eight-year-olds in tow,
marooned in rubber boots: "How many?" "Seven."
The beans were solid seeded, ten inch row.

No dog. The fathers, heroes to little kids
who watched those doves downed into trackless crop,
welcome an old handler who calmly bids
a trained retriever to each dead bird drop.

Feeney, wasted after his fifteenth dove,
rolled out of his kennel with a groan,
but children are his rarely sated love,
and each forsaken dove, he makes their own.

VI. Harvest Moon

A year ago Steve saw me in seizure's throes
and told his wife he'd bidden goodbye to Tim.
Frank Miller gave me the last rites, and Frank knows,
Christ's priest that he is, when eyes go dim,
pulse slows, blue takes the fingers and the toes,
pray for the soul.
                                        Tonight a full moon rose
and sang over my head a harvest hymn.

The Chase

Now then, Glaucon, we must post ourselves (we philosophers)
like a ring of huntsmen around the thicket, with very alert minds,
so that justice does not escape us by evaporating before us.

The Republic (432b)

I. November 24

I whirl at the faint thunder of the flush,
snap off the safety, plant my backfoot boot,
   shoulder the gun but do not shoot.
One wing flails feebly in the falling hush

as the bird swerves across the frozen bog.
It flaps about five rods, glides to the ground,
   leaps skyward with a second bound
foiled by the canines of an airborne dog.

Here is the cock I winged two weeks before,
its crop crammed full of leavings from the corn,
   its loss a disappointment borne,
but bird in mouth, the settling of a score.

The neck snapped is a mercy long deferred.
When our Alberta clippers start to blow
   no slow starvation in the snow,
no fox or coyote will consume this bird.

I bear our trophy to the truck in bliss,
the proud retriever frisking at my knees.
   Glaucon hunting with Socrates
could hardly have been happier than this.

II. December 8

Cascading from the cropland's terraced shelf,
the sidehill western wheatgrass rolls away
and the seedheads of sideoats grama sway,
descending to the deadend basin's shore.
The closest roadhead is a mile or more.
"Think like a rooster, Tim," I tell myself.

Black-eyed susans have colonized the slopes,
feral reminders of the sunflower fields
abandoned when the weevils halved our yields.
in the foodplots whose flanking grasses drain
to clumps of cattail topped by feathery cane
two practiced predators repose their hopes.

Windward we work to maximize surprise.
Four miles into this prairie white with hoar
Feeney pounces. Two lurking roosters soar
and fall victim to stamina and stealth,
weighting my vest with other-worldly wealth,
a pair of cocks purloined in paradise.

Contemplating the eldest of our arts,
I gut the birds and feed my friend their hearts.

III. December 15

I pick my slow way past the pockmarked sedge
where calves have kicked their divots,
then climb to hunt the upland's grassy edge
rounding the center pivots
whose verdant verge I choose to stalk.
There breakfast lies within a rooster's walk.

The prairie is a poem rarely read.
Its looseleaf pages blow.
Too many students of this landscape fled
its poverty and snow.
Today I limp on stiffening knees,
hoping that heedless pheasants take their ease

in pigeon grasses sprung from durum stubble,
in fragrant cedar shadow
where a boy watched his father down a double.
Maker of marsh and meadow,
grant me more time to understand,
more years to walk and memorize this land.

NOTES

The Chase: The quote from The Republic is the English translation of Ortega y Gasset's own translation from Plato in *Meditations on Hunting.*

Ecce Canis: Behold the dog.

Agápē: The love of God for man or man for God. *Te Dominus amat*: God loves you.

Disenchantment Bay: Bergy bits are small icebergs; brash, shattered ice.

Wind River Justice: *Lykos* is Greek for wolf.

Two Hands Prairie: *El Rio de las Animas Perdidas in Purgatorio*, the river of the lost souls in Purgatory. In southeast Colorado, it is now known as The Purgatory.

Jornada del Muerto: Dead Man's Walk, the title of a McMurtry novel.

INDEX OF TITLES AND FIRST LINES

ACKNOWLEDGEMENTS

I thank the editors of the publications which published these poems from *Mortal Stakes* and *Faint Thunder*:

Hudson Review, The Doorman, VIP Lounge, Dodwells Road, The Chase, Hunter's Log, Cold Front, Case Notes

The Formalist, Unnatural Selection, End of the Line, Tide Race, How Shall I Drink?

Chronicles, Words for my Forebear, Peder Anders Sulerud, Riderless Horses, *Ecce Canis,* Huntress, Soul of the North, Missing Mass, Mission Church, *Fin de Saison*

The Dark Horse, Ischemic Event, Remission, Missouri Breaks, Cross-lashed

The New Criterion, Cole, Three Kites

Light Quarterly, The Great Moorhead Fire, Prayer for the Bushmills, Too Old for this Game, Booker's Luck, Checklist, Red State Reveille, Some Assembly Required

Poetry, Mortal Stakes, *Agápē,* Disenchantment Bay, Prison Chaplain

First Things, Father Peter, Nine Bells, Wisdom, No Turning Back, In David's Line, Confessiones, Farm Boy Call Kayla, Wind River Justice, Georgic, Flight to Murdo

Shit Creek Review, Bull Rider, Cross and Veil, Snowgeese, Two Miles West, The Bowline, Prayer for a Horseman

Chimaera, Too Old for this Game, *Swa Hit Aeror Waes,* Conestoga Bark, Robert Ward, *Agnostica,* Classmate

Lucid Rhythms, Manly Arts

The Raintown Review, Liferaft, St. Paul on his Feastday, *Lux et Tenebrae,* To the Chief Musician, High Over Oahe, *Ad Te Domine,* Two Hands Prairie

The Flea, The Seven, *Priere pour deux,* Aaron Poochigian, The Reading

Gray's Sporting Journal, The Blind Retrieve, Posted, The Brummond Quarter, Rhymes From the Rosebud

Able Muse, The West

Umbrella, The Lady and the Greyhound

Measure, The Ladies at Kent Island

Lavender Review, Night Flight

The following poems appeared in these anthologies: Bull Rider in Filled With Breath, Exot Press. Case Notes in The Penguin Pocket Anthology of Modern American Poetry. *Confessiones* in Grace Notes, published by First Things.

Born in 1951, Timothy Murphy grew up in the Red River Valley of the North. Since he was graduated from Yale College as Scholar of the House in Poetry in 1972, he has farmed and hunted in the Dakotas. His previous collections of poetry are *The Deed of Gift,* Story Line Press, 1998, and *Very Far North,* Waywiser Press, 2002. His memoir in verse and prose, *Set the Ploughshare Deep,* was published by Ohio University Press in 2002. With his late partner, Alan Sullivan, he translated the *Beowulf,* which AB Longman published in 2004.